Count to 100 with the NBA!

SCHOLASTIC INC.

New York   Toronto   London   Auckland   Sydney
Mexico City   New Delhi   Hong Kong   Buenos Aires

1 Flying Mascot

2 Resting Players

Tracy McGrady
Grant Hill

3 Shiny Trophies

4
Jumping Legs

Vince Carter
Allen Iverson

Gimme 5!

Latrell Sprewell
Allan Houston

6

Feet of Power

6ft.

5ft.

4ft.

3ft.

2ft.

1ft.

Andre Mille

7 Feet for Dunking

Kevin Garnett

7 ft.

6 ft.

5 ft.

4 ft.

3 ft.

2 ft.

1 ft.

8 Orange Cones

Jersey Number

George Lynch

Kobe Bryant
Shaquille O'Neal

10

Winning Fingers

11 12 13

14 15 16

17 18 19.

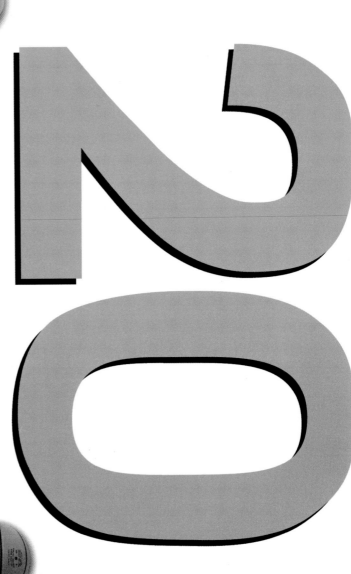

Karl Malone

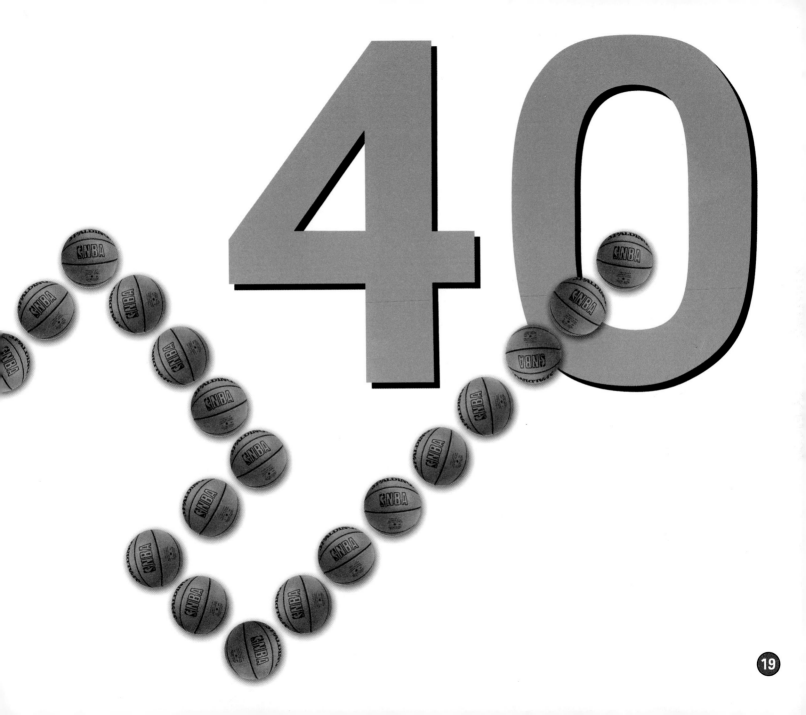

Antawn Jamison

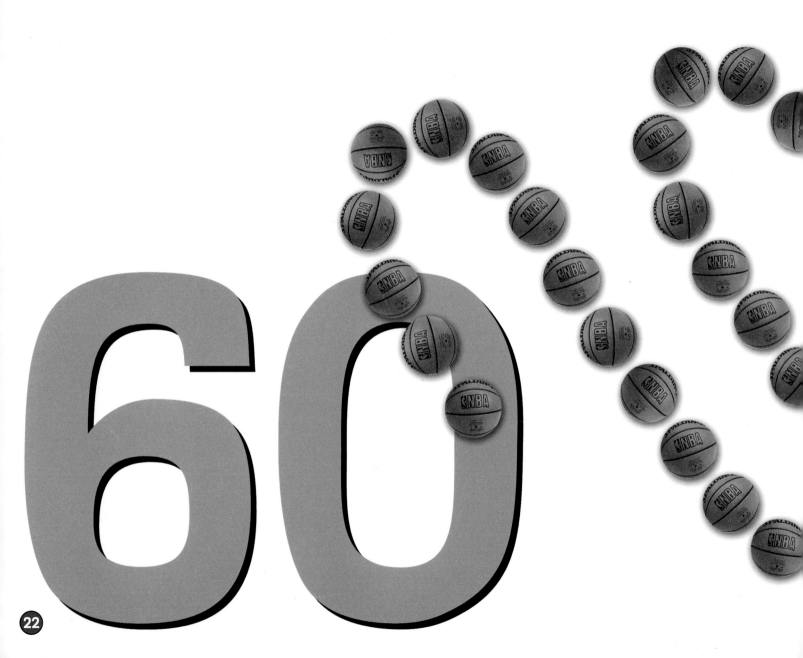

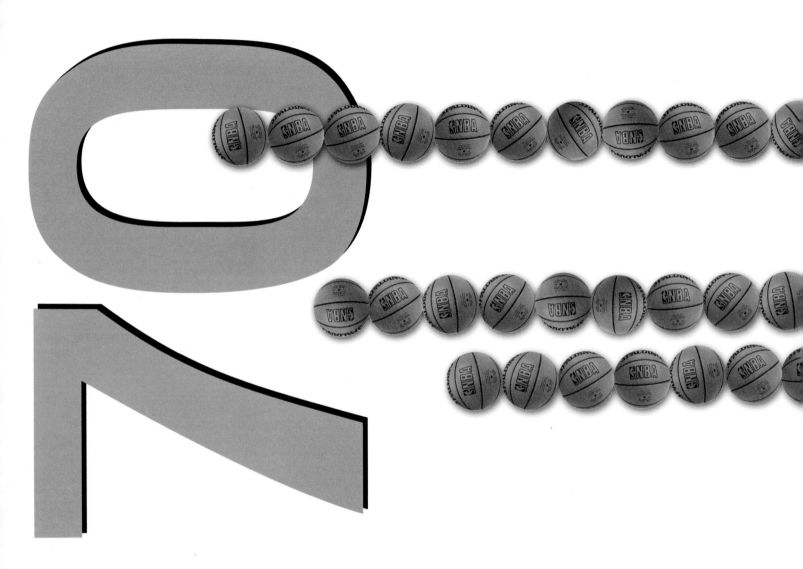

Glenn Robinson

Shawn Marion

Wilt Chamberlain scored 100 points in a single game!